W9-CAZ-298

18

**Discovering
Cultures**

India

Patricia J. Murphy

Benchmark Books

MARSHALL CAVENDISH
NEW YORK

For the children of India—P.J.M.

With thanks to Bindu Bhatt, South Asian Studies Librarian, Columbia University, for the careful review of this manuscript.

Benchmark Books
Marshall Cavendish
99 White Plains Road
Tarrytown, New York 10591-9001
www.marshallcavendish.com

All Internet sites were available and accurate when sent to press.

Library of Congress Cataloging-in-Publication Data

Murphy, Patricia J., 1963–
India / by Patricia J. Murphy.
p. cm. — (Discovering cultures)
Summary: Highlights the geography, people, food, schools, recreation, celebrations, and languages of India, the largest country in South Asia.
Includes bibliographical references and index.
ISBN 0-7614-1516-5
1. India—Juvenile literature. [1. India.] I. Title. II. Series.
DS407 .M87 2003
954—dc21   2002015306

Photo Research by Candlepants Incorporated
Front Cover Photo: Dinodia Picture Agency/Ravi Shekhar

The photographs in this book are used by permission and through the courtesy of; *Dinodia Picture Agency*: Debashish Banerjee, 1; N.G. Sharma, 4-5, 8-9; Sudip Bhaumik, 6; Jagdish Agarwal,10, 34 (lower) 42 (lower); Ravi Shekhar,13, 20-21, 29(left), 34(top), 39; Manoj Navalkar, 14; V.H. Mishra, 15; Milind Ketkar,16, 28, 33, 40, back cover; Viren Desal, 17; B.D. Rupani, 18; Madhusudan Tawde, 19, 30; Pradip Gupta, 21(right); Sharad J. Devare, 22-23; Hari Mahidhar, 24 (left), 24-25; Mahendra Patil, 26(left); Umesh Gogna, 26(right); R.J. Productions, 29(right); Rajesh Vora, 31; Vishwanath Mishra, 32; M. Amirtham, 35; Suraj Sharma, 36-37; Pramod Mistry, 38; Anil Dave, 41. *Getty Images/Hulton Archive*: 42(top), 43.

Map and illustrations by Salvatore Murdocca
Book design by Virginia Pope

Cover: *The Taj Mahal*; Title page: *Indian woman in traditional dress*

Printed in Hong Kong
1 3 5 6 4 2

Turn the Pages...

Put your hands together.
Point your fingers up. Bow
forward. Say, *"Namaste!"*
You have just greeted
someone the Indian way.
Namaste means
"I respect you."

Come along and discover
more about the people and
culture of India.

Indian children at play

Where in the World Is India?

The Republic of India is the largest country in South Asia. It is also the seventh largest country in the world. It is believed that long ago India was part of a much larger continent called Gondwanaland. When the continent broke apart, India headed north. It bumped right into Asia! Because India is so large, it is called a subcontinent.

Shaped like a triangle, India is a peninsula. It is surrounded by water on three sides. The Arabian Sea lies to the west with the Indian Ocean to the South. New Delhi, India's modern capital city, is located in the northern part of the country. Some of India's neighbors include China, Afghanistan, and Pakistan.

India's highest mountain, Kanchenjunga

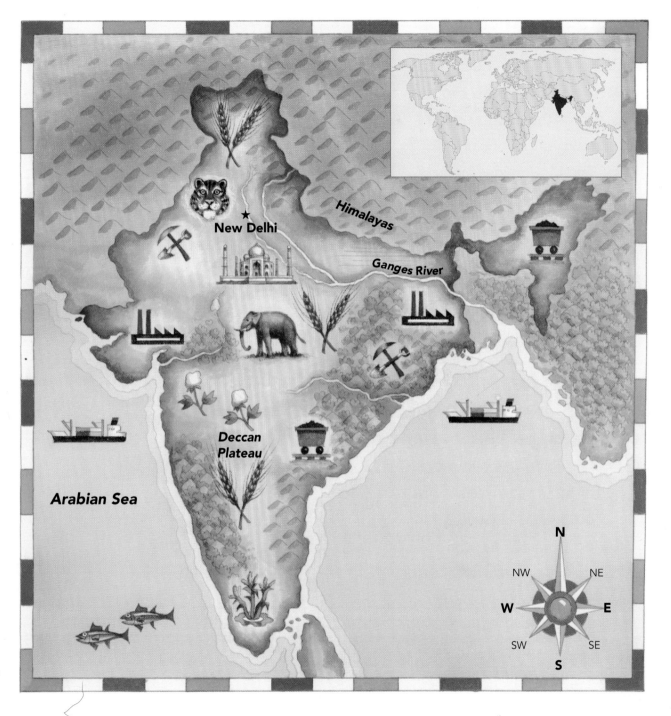

New Delhi

Himalayas

Ganges River

Deccan
Plateau

Arabian Sea

N
NW   NE
W   E
SW   SE
S

India's landscape changes from place to place. In the north, mountains cross the country. India's mountain ranges include the Himalaya Mountains. The second largest river, the Ganges, begins in India's Himalayas. It is 1,500 miles (2,413 kilometers) long. Kanchenjunga, India's highest peak, is also found in the Himalayas.

Moving south, India's landforms include the Indo-Gangetic Plain and the Deccan Plateau. The Indo-Gangetic Plain runs along the Indus and Ganges rivers. This rich, fertile land is perfect for growing India's main crops including rice and grain. It is also where most Indians live.

The Ganges River

India's Bengal tiger

The Deccan Plateau is an area of high, flat land. Much of India's wildlife such as the Bengal tiger, one-horned rhinoceros, and the Indian elephant roam on the Deccan Plateau. India's tropical rain forests are alive with some of the world's most unusual plants and animals. It is wet and colorful. The subcontinent's deserts are dry, sandy, and very hot.

India is located near the equator. Countries near the equator are closest to the sun. They receive the sun's

High atop the Deccan Plateau

Monsoon season

strongest rays. That means it gets very hot in India. However, India's temperatures can vary from the cold, snow-covered peaks of the Himalayas to the hot, steamy rain forests.

In June and July, the summer monsoon brings rain to India. Monsoons are powerful storms that sweep across the country from the Indian Ocean. Their moist air and strong winds cause heavy rainfall. Monsoons provide the rain needed for farming, but they also bring deadly floods. Cyclones, dust storms, hailstorms, and earthquakes also hit many parts of the country.

The Ganges River

Indians love water. Water helps their crops grow. It also cleans their bodies
and their souls. Indians believe the Ganges River once flowed from the heavens.
They believe its waters are sacred. Because of this, many Indians take pilgrimages
to the Ganges River. They drink the water from the Ganges. They bathe in the
river and scatter the ashes of their dead in it. Indians believe the sacred
water will wash away their bad deeds. And when they die, they
believe it will lead them to a holy resting place.

What Makes India Indian?

India is like a colorful painting with many bright colors. It is a country of different people, religions, languages, and ways of life. India is made up of twenty-nine separate states and six territories. Each of India's states is like its own country. They have their own languages, customs, traditions, and festivals.

The official languages of India are Hindi and English. English is used mostly in government and business matters. There are also many other recognized languages and over a thousand dialects or local languages.

Religion is the center of Indian life. Eighty percent of Indians follow a religion called Hinduism. They are known as Hindus. Hindus are a very religious people. They pray to God in many different forms and call God many different names. The rest of India's

Worshipers at India's Golden Temple

people follow other religions such as Islam, Buddhism, Jainism, Sikhism, Christianity, or Judaism.

Hinduism is a way of life. Hindus believe they must not hurt any living thing.

Daily prayer

That is why many Hindus do not eat meat. They also believe that when a person dies, he is soon reborn. This is called reincarnation.

Many Hindus believe that people are born into social groups called castes. Castes have special rules. These rules determine where people will live and what jobs they will have. They also decide what friends they will have and whom they will marry. Hindus believe that a person's karma, or actions, in one life decides their fate in the next. Discrimination against people based on caste is illegal in India. However, some people still live by the caste system rules.

No matter what religion they follow or caste they are, all Indians share a deep love of family. Grandparents, aunts, uncles, cousins, moms, dads, and children may live together in the same house. Children are taught to respect

Indian families often live together in the same home.

their elders. When Indian children grow up, their families choose the people they will marry. When a girl marries, she moves into her husband's family's home.

Colorful clothes are part of Indian life. Indian women dress in traditional saris. Saris look like long dresses. They are made from long pieces of material that wrap around the body at the waist and over the shoulder. Women also decorate their foreheads with *bindis* (colorful dots) and wear shiny, dangling jewelry. Men wear

Many Indian women wear bindis, saris, and jewelry.

kurtas (shirts without collars), *churdiars* (pants), and *dhotis*. *Dhotis* are like sashes that wrap around the waist and between the legs. Some Hindu and Sikh men also wear turbans to put up their hair. Muslim men wear embroidered caps.

Indian art is as colorful as their clothing. Art is a way of life in India. It celebrates the Indians' different religions, beliefs, legends, myths, and national pride. Indians have given the world lively paintings, music, dance, architecture, and literature. Their temples, mosques, forts, and monuments are recognized for their

Indian art tells stories and legends.

beautiful architecture. And India's ancient stories and poems have been read around the world.

In the United States, people eat Indian foods like *dhal* (lentil bean soup) and *tandoori* chicken. They listen to Indian music and watch Indian movies. They use words that come from the Hindi language such as shampoo, punch, thug, and dungarees. They may also use many things from India and not even know it. The ideas for toilets, Arabic numerals (1, 2, 3, 4), algebra, yoga, chess, and pajamas all came from India.

The Taj Mahal

It took nearly twenty years, twenty thousand workers, one thousand elephants and twenty-five million dollars to build. What is it? It is the Taj Mahal.

The Taj Mahal is a monument on the banks of the Yamura River in Agra, India. It stands in honor of Mumtaz Mahal, the wife of a seventeenth-century emperor, Shah Jahan. She died at the age of thirty-nine after giving birth to their fourteenth child. Shah Jahan was very sad when his wife died. To remember her, he built this special monument around her tomb. The Taj Mahal, meaning "crown of the palace," is made of white marble and is built on a red sandstone platform. It has twenty-two domes and four towers called minarets.

The Taj Mahal is often called the eighth wonder of the world. It is one of the most popular tourist attractions in India.

Living in India

India is a country of old and new, rich and poor. It is also big and overcrowded. With more than one billion people, India has the second biggest population in the world! Only China has more people. India is just one-third the size of the United States, but it has ten times more citizens.

Some Indians live in large cities such as New Delhi, Calcutta, and Bombay. Eighty percent of Indians, however, live in small country villages. Whether they live in cities or villages, people pray throughout the day. They pray in temples, mosques, or at shrines in their homes.

New Delhi's streets are filled with bikes, rickshaws, cars, buses, markets, and people. You might even see a cow, elephant, camel, or monkey. Those who live in the city live in apartments or houses.

The city of Delhi

Air pollution in an Indian city

They have electricity and running water. Many work in India's growing computer software, manufacturing, tourism, or textile industries.

In crowded cities there are many problems. There are not enough homes or jobs for the people who need them. Many people who

leave the village for the city end up living in the slums or on the streets. Indian cities also have serious problems such as air and water pollution, and shortages of electricity and food. These problems can cause disease and death.

In villages, most Indian families farm the land. India's main crops are rice, grains, sugar, spices, tea, cashews, cotton, potatoes, and jute oil. Many farmers grow wheat, beans, and chickpeas. Others grow fruits, vegetables, spices, tobacco, sugar, or cotton. Along the water, fishermen catch mackerel, sardines, shrimp, carp, and catfish. Miners pull iron, coal, gas, oil, diamonds, and other minerals from the ground. Indian artists make handicrafts like pottery, baskets, metalwork, carpets, silk, or other fabrics.

Many villagers live in one-room houses made from brick, mud, straw, or grass. These homes have dirt or tiled

At work in the village

Relaxing on a charpoy

floors, small kitchens, and open-air spaces to visit. Most of them do not have running water, electricity, or furniture. Indians may sit and eat on mats, and lie on small beds called *charpoys*.

A house made of straw and mud

Indians cook their meals on small stoves inside their kitchens. They use lots of curry to flavor their food. Curry is a blend of many different spices. It makes everything a bit spicier and hotter. Most Indian meals combine rice, grains, lentils, vegetables, and yogurt with meat or fish and flat bread called *chapati*. People drink coffee, tea, or *lassi*. After meals, they also enjoy sweets like *burfee*, sherbets, and fruit juices.

An Indian meal and burfees

Let's Eat!
Mango Lassi

Want something smooth and sweet? Try some Mango Lassi. It is a lot like a milkshake. Ask an adult to help you prepare this popular Indian drink.

Ingredients:

1 cup plain yogurt

$1/3$ cup canned mango pulp

$1/2$ cup ice

Wash your hands. Gather and measure all of your ingredients. Pour ingredients into an electric blender. Blend them together for about one minute. Pour into glasses. Makes two 8-ounce servings.

School Days

A good education is an Indian child's ticket to a bright future. The Indian government requires all children ages six to fourteen to attend primary school. In India, primary school is free. Children study grammar, spelling, social studies, math, science, history, and Hindi.

After completing primary school, students ages fourteen to eighteen may attend India's secondary schools, or high schools. In high school, students take classes such as English, math, science, chemistry, biology, history, and economics. Those who do well in high school may study science, technology, business, or the arts at India's colleges or universities.

City schools are very different from those in villages. City children learn in

Some Indian children ride buses to school.

Indoor and outdoor classrooms

brick buildings with windows. There are desks, seats, and books for every student. Some students pay to attend private schools. Private schools are expensive.

In some villages, there are no buildings for schools. School may be held under a tree. There are few books or supplies. Many village children do not attend school. Their families are too poor. They cannot afford paper, pencils, books, and uniforms. Instead of going to school, these children work in family farms or businesses. Some village children may attend boarding schools far away from home.

After school, Indian children love to play!

In many areas of India, fewer girls attend school than boys. Their families think that they do not need school. They believe girls should be at home taking care of the family. These beliefs, however, are changing. Many more girls are attending high school and college. India's government is working to create better schools for all children. This will only mean a brighter future for India.

Friendship Bands

Indian children like to make friendship bands. You can make some for your friends, too.

Materials:

Different color cotton or satin threads, 1/4 inch wide

Scissors

Directions:

1. Cut three 8-inch strands of colored thread. Tie the three strands together with a knot 1/2 inch from the end of the threads.

2. Braid the strands one color at a time.

3. Continue braiding until you are 1/2 inch away from the end of the threads. Tie a knot.

4. Wrap the band around a friend's wrist.

5. Tie the two ends of the band together.

6. Trade friendship bands with all of your friends!

Just for Fun

Indians like fun and games. They enjoy sharing the latest news and telling stories including Indian myths and legends. Their stories may be told with puppets or through songs. Indians also like playing cards and games with families, neighbors, and friends. Board games like chess and *pachisi* (Parcheesi) are two favorites. Indian children fly kites, shoot marbles, and play sports. Children in villages make toys out of things they find. Some make little clay dolls shaped into Hindu gods and goddesses.

Citizens and tourists hike, bike, and explore India's mountain ranges. Its shores are popular places to swim, boat, fish, or just splash around. Many people visit India's famous attractions

Shooting marbles

such as the Taj Mahal and ancient ruins. Others journey to the holy waters of the Ganges River and the Buddhist Temple at Bodh Gayá. Still others visit Indian amusement parks, national parks, and conservatories.

Indians are great sports fans. They love to watch and play many sports. Cricket, soccer, field hockey, wrestling, and polo are India's favorite sports. Cricket is played on a field with eleven players on each team. It is a lot like baseball. Players use bats, balls, and bases called wickets. Polo is like field hockey played on horseback. Players use long, wooden mallets to hit a

An Indian amusement park

A polo match

small ball. Many Indians perform martial arts and yoga. Yoga exercises relax the body and the mind.

In Indian cities, people love to shop in market-places and watch Indian movies. The city of Bombay is often called Bollywood. It is like Hollywood in the United States. Bollywood is the leading producer of motion pictures in the world. It films as many as 800 movies a year! Many are love stories and dramas. They are favorites in India and throughout the world.

Practicing yoga

Kabaddi

Do you like to play tag? Well, so do teenage boys and girls—and many men—in India. Their game is called Kabaddi and it is a whole lot rougher! Kabaddi is played on a field 40 feet (12 meters) long by 25–32 feet (8–10 meters) wide. A line, called a middle line, divides the court in half.

To begin, a player, or raider, from one team must run across the middle line. His goal is to tag as many players, or anti-raiders, from the other team as he can. Then he must return to his side of the field while holding his breath!

To make sure that he does not take a breath, he must say over and over, "Kabbadi, Kabbadi, Kabbadi!" Anti-raiders try to tackle the raider before he crosses the middle line and returns to his side of the court. If the raider takes a breath or is tackled by the anti-raiders, he is out. If he does not take a breath, he earns his team ten points for every anti-raider that he tagged. At the end of the game, the team with the most points wins—and everyone breathes easier!

Let's Celebrate!

Indians follow a lunar, or moon, calendar. On this calendar, they observe hundreds of holidays and festivals each year. Many of these celebrations mark changes in the seasons or recall special events in India's history. Others honor religious gods and prophets. Indians also celebrate weddings and birthdays. All of these celebrations allow families and friends to share customs and traditions. With so many special occasions each year, it is no wonder there is something to celebrate almost every day in India!

India's Republic Day and Independence Day show Indian pride. On January 26, Indians celebrate the day that India became a republic. They celebrate Republic Day with feasts, fairs, and parades. Indian Independence Day is observed on August 15. On this day, Indians remember their country's struggle to be free from British rule. Indians celebrate by waving Indian flags, singing the national anthem, and listening to speeches.

Many of India's religious holidays begin with fasting and end with feasting! Most of these days are filled with bright

Elephants march in a Republic Day parade.

36

Holiday fireworks

colors, spicy food, lively music, dance, and parades. Some are fun and festive like the Hindu celebrations of Diwali, Holi, and Raksha Bandhan.

Diwali is the Hindu festival of lights. It lasts five days. It comes at the end of the monsoon season when the rainy season crops have been harvested. It usually falls in October or November on a night with a new moon. During Diwali, everything seems to glow. Hindu temples, homes, public places, and streams are lit with thousands of oil or electric lamps. Some Hindus believe that these lights will

Holi festival fun

lead Lakshmi, the Hindu goddess of wealth and good fortune, to their doors. Families prepare for Diwali by cleaning and decorating. They buy new clothes to wear and prepare large feasts. The holiday ends the way it began—with light! Fireworks brighten up Indian skies.

The spring festival of Holi is a lot like April Fool's Day—only messier! It is held in February or March when there is a bright, full moon. During Holi, people young and old play tricks on one another. They splash colored water and throw colored powder on one another. Bonfires are also set. Holi's festivities celebrate the end of winter and the beginning of spring, as well as the triumph of good over evil.

A brother and sister celebrate Raksha Bandhan.

Raksha Bandhan celebrates the special relationship between brothers and sisters. On this day, a sister ties a colorful bracelet of silky threads, called a *rakhi*, on her brother's wrist. The bracelet represents his vow of protection. Once he receives the bracelet, he promises to always protect her from harm.

The Muslim holiday of Ramadan takes up the whole ninth month of the Muslim calendar. It is a time filled with prayer and fasting. Muslims do not eat from sunrise to sunset for thirty days. They fast to honor those who have less than them. They believe fasting builds strength. When Ramadan is over, Muslims celebrate Id-ul-Fitr. It is the day that ends the fasting. It is celebrated with music and dancing—and eating!

Mehndi

India is a land of colorful decoration. Indian women are no different! They adorn their bodies with brightly colored saris and shiny jewelry. They also like to decorate their bodies with *mehndi*. *Mehndi* is body painting. It is applied to the hands and feet for weddings, special events, and festivals.

Mehndi artists use ink made from ground henna leaves and oil. The ink is squeezed through a plastic tube. Sometimes, these artists use stencils to make their flowery designs. Other times, they do them freehand. These designs take many hours to apply. They are set with a layer of lemon juice. When the artists are done, *mehndi* designs looks like lace gloves and stockings. They last about two weeks. *Mehndi* designs are very beautiful. It is just too bad that they do not last longer!

India's flag has three stripes. They are saffron (yellow-orange), white, and green. Saffron represents strength. Green represents India's rich, fertile land. White represents peace. A symbol of the Ashoka Chakra is in the center of the white stripe. It is a blue wheel. It is India's wheel of law. The flag was adopted in July of 1947.

India's money is called the rupee. The exchange rate often changes, but 48.4 rupees equaled one U.S. dollar in 2002.

Count in Hindi

English	Hindi	Say it like this:
one	एक	ACHE
two	दो	DOUGH
three	तीन	TEEN
four	चार	CHARR
five	पाँच	PAUNCH
six	छे	CHAY
seven	सात	SOT
eight	आठ	ART
nine	नौ	NOW
ten	दस	DUSS

Glossary

burfee Candy made with milk, nuts, dried fruit, and flavorings.

caste (KAST) Social group that determines where people will live and work.

fasting To give up or stop eating for a time, usually done during certain holidays.

henna A green plant; its leaves are crushed and used to make mehndi designs.

lassi Cool drink made with fruit and yogurt.

mosque (MOSK) Building used for worship by Muslims.

namaste (na-ma-STAY) Hindi greeting meaning "I respect you" or "I bow to you."

republic Country that has its own form of government.

rickshaw Two- or three-wheeled hooded vehicle pulled or cycled by one person.

subcontinent Large land mass that is part of a continent.

Proud to Be Indian

Mohandas K. Gandhi (1869–1948)

Gandhi was born on October 2, 1869 in Porbandar, India. People in India called him Mahatma Gandhi. Mahatma means "great soul." Gandhi earned this name because of the peaceful ways that he solved problems. He helped India become free from British rule with peaceful protests. He asked Indians to stop buying British-made goods and to make their own. He also fought against the caste system. He called his way *Satyagraha* or the force of truth. Gandhi believed that anything done with violence was wrong. But not everyone agreed with him. He was shot to death in 1948.

Mother Teresa (1910–1997)

Mother Teresa was born in Skopje, Yugoslavia in 1910. Although she was not Indian, she was considered a very special Indian resident. Mother Teresa spent most of her life in India helping people in need. For thirty years, she worked with the very sick and needy people of Calcutta, India. She helped open hospitals, schools, shelters, and orphanages. She started her own order or group of nuns called the Missionaries of Charity. She also received medical training. She opened a shelter for orphans and very sick people. Others throughout the world joined her work. Mother Teresa earned a Nobel Peace Prize in 1979 in honor of her work. She died in 1997.

Rudyard Kipling (1865–1936)

Rudyard Kipling was born in Bombay, India on December 30, 1865. When he was young, he attended school in England. Upon completing school, Kipling returned to India. He began to write stories for an Indian newspaper. He also started to write short stories, poems, and novels. His first collection of poems was published in 1886. Two of his most famous books were *Kim* (a novel) and *The Jungle Book*. *The Jungle Book* became a popular children's book. It was also made into a Disney movie in the 1960s. Kipling won the Nobel Prize for Literature in 1907. He died in 1936.

Find Out More

Books

Look What Came from India by Miles Harvey. Franklin Watts, New York, 1999.

Colors of India by Holly Littlefield. Carolrhoda Books, Inc., Minnesota, 2000.

India by Joanne Mattern. Bridgestone Books, Minnesota, 2003.

Look What We Brought You from India by Phyllis Shalant. Simon & Schuster, New York, 1998.

Web sites

Pitara for Kids
http://www.pitara.com

Indian Embassy
http://www.indianembassy.org

Tour India
http://www.tourindia.com

Video

Lords of the Animals: Chami and Ana the Elephant. The Phoenix Learning Group, Missouri, 1995. VHS; 26 min.

Index

Page numbers for illustrations are in **boldface.**

About the Author

Patricia J. Murphy writes children's story-books, nonfiction books, early readers, and poetry. She also writes for magazines, corporations, educational publishing companies, and museums.

Patricia lives in Northbrook, IL, USA. She enjoys Indian music, movies, and food—especially lentil spreads on warm bread! She also has three Indian cousins named Sonjay, Rohan, and Gina.

Acknowledgments

Special thanks to the Indian Embassy in Washington, D.C., the India Tourism Bureau, and the diverse people of India who were so interesting to write about!